My People's Freedom

J H Bayliss Frederick

Artnell
Publishing

My People's Freedom

Artnell Publishing, Florida, USA

ISBN: 978-0-990-90830-2

Dedicated to the memory of
John Sardona and Constance Bayliss

"Next in importance to freedom and justice is popular education, without which neither freedom nor justice can be permanently maintained."

James A Garfield (1831 to 1881)

Contents

My People's Freedom

Chapter One

Little John Baily

They call me by several names all to which I, to this day, answer in response. But I was actually christened 'John' by the priest when my mother called me 'Baily', her father's surname. Pa persisted in calling me 'Bully'. He wanted a son who could fight and be respected and feared in the village. My aunt and grandmother insisted on having me called 'Bonny'.

They say I was the prettiest baby of the village and all the villagers affectionately called me 'Brother B'. At elementary school they wrote 'John', and at secondary school they wrote and called me 'John Baily'. After secondary I am called by, and I answer to, anything.

My father was and is the only 'Jack of all trades' I have ever known. He was a 'smith' - farrier, black, tin and silver. I never saw him work gold. He was carpenter, mason, rigger, a sought-after toolmaker and an excellent painter. He constructed buildings that looked as if they could last forever. He handled metals and was also a gunsmith and an emergency dentist. He crudely extracted pain-giving teeth at sixpence per tooth. Over and above he was an engineering draughtsman and built, as a construction contractor, from a horse-drawn buggy to the body of a coach and from a church to cocoa sweat-houses and drying sheds on railway tracks for the estates.

From 1930 up to 1946 he practised as a construction contractor and died broken-hearted by reason of punishment for what was termed rudeness to the authorities, including the estate owners.

The southern shore of the island of Tobaccoc is a series of inlets, all beautiful, sandy beaches. My village with its two sandy beaches lay between Bigwood and Goldtown on the west, and Glenmorgin, Richland and Gardenville on the east. We in Brookeville were the poorest. We existed for the agricultural estates in this segment of the island. The importance of the village and as a consequence, the villagers, depended on the volume and value of agricultural produce for shipment overseas. Inter-village rivalry was based on the value and quantity of exports to England.

There was one courthouse six miles away and one police station with one lame corporal and four constables.

The courthouse served the eastern half of the island, twelve miles from Bigwood to Charlotte, the farthest village east; the police station served the same expanse.

One medical doctor, one district nurse, one sanitary inspector and teachers for three elementary schools completed the civil staffing of government facilities.

At the top of the island's community pyramid was the warden, an Englishman, then the all-white estate owners; next were the police inspector, magistrate and doctor who were also from England. All other humans were black

5

people whose parents were slaves from Africa. There were no Chinese, Syrians, Americans or Indians.

The estates were owned by white people holding title by a crown grant from Queen Victoria for service to the Empire. These gentlemen were usually non-residents. In our island there existed a white managerial class. Below these were the bookkeepers, the overseers and charge-hands ably supported by the heads of all government departments: Prisons, Courts, Hospital, Schools, Police, Education and Public Works - all white appointees from England.

Only white people owned land in Tobaccoc. Black people could rent a piece of land, a small piece, and if the house he built was too large or too pretty the white land-owner gave him a "notiss to squit." The rent was paid partly in labour on the estate.

What kept the society stable and functioning in its own way was common suffering, open discrimination and an inherent uniting love for one another.

The children all belonged to the whole community and discipline was administered by all to all. All shared everything with everybody. Everyone looked after the aged of the community. The struggles of one were the struggles of all.

I remember events, incidents and things from age three years. Our house was about three hundred yards from the Anglican schoolhouse. With and most times without clothes on, I entered the classes and left at will. Nobody put me out or complained. So at age four, I was enrolled in the third-stage infants class and that very year I was skipped over standard one into standard two. I was a very fast learner.

But with learning, I acquired confusion of mind. I could not understand why the teachers showed deference to the children of light complexion, or why us, the black children, did the sweeping and cleaning of the school and the light-skinned did nothing but laugh and make fun of us. Why the black ones sat at the back of the class and the brown-skinned ones to the front. Why the estate owners' children never came over to our school. Why the God we were told of at Sunday School was not a fair God. Why the pews from the middle of the church right up to the row before the altar were rented to the estate owners who came to service only at Christmas and Easter, and why God allowed the white people to always have plenty of money while all of us, the black people, had nothing.

My mother persistently and up to the time of her death lectured my brothers, sisters and me, "You have to give up your rights for peace and Jesus' sake." But she never made such comments to or even in the hearing of Pa. He, Pa, was a staunch Roman Catholic who said many things disloyal to the church whenever treatment of black people became topical. At those times or on those occasions my father bewailed his lack of power to rectify or change what he moaningly described as, "That can't be right."

So when Cartright Rubli, the acolyte to Father Stack at Bigwood Catholic Church, was sent to jail for catching a deer in his, Cartright's contract plot at Goldtown Estate, Pa told nearly everybody from Bigwood to Gardenville how, "That can't be right." Pa explained that wild animals belong only to God, and whoever catches one becomes the owner of it.

And Pa blamed Father Stack, he being a priest from Ireland and the magistrate's friend, for not going to Court to talk up for Cartright. All the villages' people remembered the pay-evening at Goldtown Estate's yard when Cartright argued with Mr Gall, the estate owner, for keeping back one day's pay out of his week's wage because Mr Gall had sent him to town during the week to fetch a suitcase from the steamer's office for Mrs Gall. Cartright took a whole day to walk the twenty-four miles. He shed tears crying out to Mr Gall that the reason he wasn't quicker was the hot sun. The grip was heavy so he, Cartright, only stopped to drink some water and eat a piece of food that Ma Nancy gave him when he got to Mount George. All the labourers groaned aloud in sympathy with Cartright and Mr Gall called him back and paid him the sixpence that was the missing day's pay.

My father and all the labourers say that Mr Gall reported to the rural constable that the deer was his so the rural constable put on his badge, took his staff and Cartright, under arrest, six miles to the police station at Rex Hill. Cartright spent two days in the prisoner cell and the next day Mr Meeden, the magistrate, stopped in at Mr Gall's great house on the way to court at Rex Hill. They say they never saw a case done so quickly as Cartright's case.

Pa himself told us at home how Meeden walked in the Courthouse, picked up a sheet of paper and called out, "Cartright Rubli."

The police corporal shouted out, "Present Sah!" and pushed Cartright to stand up in the space in front of Meeden.

Meeden read out, "Cartright Rubli you are charged for stealing one deer, the property of Goldtown Estate. You are guilty?"

Cartright answered, trembling like a leaf, "I catch the deer in my garden, eating my sweet potato vine. It was a wild deer come over the mountain."

The magistrate in a vexed voice said, "You ignorant people cannot understand that what is on a man's land belongs to him. The deer was on Mr Gall's land. The deer belonged to Mr Gall and you tell me you catch it in your garden. Your garden is on Mr Gall's land. Is it so?"

Cartright answered, "Yes Sah."

Then Meeden called out almost shouting, "You are guilty.

You'll go to jail for fourteen days, hard labour."

Pa nearly choked with rage as he finished speaking. My bigger brother said, "Black people don't get any justice."

Ma gave him a slap across the mouth. Although it didn't bleed, Pa rushed at her with his right hand lifted and as if to strike her.

He didn't, but said gesturing helplessly, "Well if you are teaching these children to be stupid people," and walked away.

Chapter Two

~

Something 'Ain't Right'

My world, then, consisted of my immediate family and our environment - the surroundings and people with whom we daily came into contact, and a God above who looked down, insisting that everything was good and who punished everything that was bad. Pa was next after God, then Ma, and then my bigger brother.

Often, under the sapodilla tree on the far side of the donkey stable, I would sit and dream of an army made up of Pa, leading my two brothers and myself, going about the village to rectify the wrongs.

Pa kept complaining how he would start with repairing Miss Deveen's house roof that high winds tore off. She, Ma says, Miss Deveen, lost her husband and her two sons who went fishing and had not returned for over one whole year now.

Then, Pa said, she began to curse nasty words because she got lonely and nobody cared. Only Ma would go and talk with her sometimes. She didn't have any family on the island. Whenever Ma went to visit a villager, Pa would smile for a long time if it were somebody old and helpless. If she carried food or a flour-bag sheet Pa would mutter, "Hmmm, good, good." And Pa would say over and over again as if it took saying something over and over for Ma to hear, "When you give to the needy, God gives you plenty, plenty more for you and them."

A six-year-old boy loves his mother most, then his sisters, then his brothers, but all along he idolizes his father. He looks to his father for answers, advice, guidance and power, physical power. The father is prophet, priest, king and leader all rolled into an infallible teacher. And so every time Pa said that something 'ain't right', I would for days be asking myself, Ma, my bigger brother and Pa himself why whatever it was that wasn't right, wasn't right. My confusion persisted. What I was told at Sunday School, what the teachers told us at school, what Ma told me at home and when we went to the garden, what I saw for myself, and what the boys at school talked about, left me doubting and not sure of anything.

Ecclesiasticus Meek was our Sunday School head teacher. We used to describe him to each other as Izze. His correct name we found too long to call. But, he taught us at Sunday School that God made all men equal and in his words, "All white man are all equal and all black man are all equal, but the white man equal in joy and us black man equal in sorrow."

When Pa would ask Ma how come the 'man of God' leaves Mrs Rodriquez's house after midnight when cock crow and how he was always staggering drunk to mount his horse when on Sunday morning he had to take service, Ma would grunt and say, "Hmm, maybe he and she deh." It took me months before the boys at school explained to me the meaning of "he and she deh." If he was God's representative in the village, then that ain't right.

I learned a song the boys at school used to sing to the big girls in senior class:

"The more we are together, together, together,

The more we are together, the merrier we shall be.

For your wife is your wife and my wife is your wife.

So the more we are together the merrier we shall be."

They said that Mr Herrick was singing that to the 'man of God' as he was having breakfast with Mrs Herrick, while Mr Herrick went out on the estate, Brookville Estate, to set tasks for the labourers. One day Mr Herrick returned earlier than expected and met them sitting on a bench in the kitchen holding hands.

Easter and Christmas were happy times. The Sundays before, you had to go to Mr Pursey's yard at Pepper Ridge to get your hair cut. The entire village went into house cleaning activities, sprucing-up bedroom, hall, kitchen and flower gardens to invite the risen Jesus at Easter, and the Baby in the manger at Christmas. Us children, from toddlers to young men and big girls, had to go around the village helping to fetch water in buckets, bowls, oil tins and bamboo joints, cut and carry firewood, sweep yards, clean drains, weed and clean flower gardens for the old people, particularly those who had no children living with them. It wasn't right if you were not loving, nice, obedient and mannerly to the older people in the whole village.

Chapter Three

The Medicine Man

During the last half of the dry season, sometime before school closed for Christmas, Pa sent me with a letter to Major Shotte, the owner of Richland Estate. Major Shotte lived in this great house overlooking Richland Bay, on a hill the slaves christened "Licks-Hill," pronounced "Liksill". Major Shotte's father, who was also an army man from England, a captain, used to whip the slaves at the back of his great house from where his wife could sit and enjoy the entertainment. Male or female was stripped, tied to a mahogany post, whipped until limp, untied and led down the hill into the sea and left there to soak the salt. When revived sufficiently the slave would shuffle to the barracks yard to join the chorus of mourners' moans.

Pa and Ti Nancy would tell us stories about slavery. My favourite is that of Mohamed, the medicine man. Ti Nancy was born a slave and Mohamed Brebnor was a slave. He, BoBo Brebnah, as he was called by the other slaves, was hurriedly freed by Major Shotte. Mohamed Brebnor's eyes, face and poised head, when he looked at you, told you he knew your past and could tell you your future. He understood and knew what was in your mind. He made people talk to you from the bushes, from behind your back or in of you, but you couldn't identify the person who spoke.

Mohamed was sold by previous owners who had grown to be afraid of him. He ended up being exchanged for a trained log-hauling ox to Captain Shotte who had just returned from the Boer's War in Africa. Major Shotte, as manager to the estate, had planted four acres of yellow yam on a slope, part of the riverbank. The yams threw out copious vines and leaves with yam leaves covering the whole area, from hilltop to river's edge. One day, Mohamed was sent by the overseer to search for bachack ants which eat the leaves of the plants and to blow up their nests, using a compound called carbide. He blew up several nests. But the next morning it alarmed all the slaves when they discovered that overnight the entire yam field was eaten by bachacks and was now clean as a whistle.

Master and overseer got hold of Mohamed, tied him up and demanded his reason for sending the bachack ants to eat the master's yams. He protested and pleaded his innocence and lack of knowledge on how to control and guide bachack. Their reply was: "Liksill for whipping."

No friends were invited, only Mrs Shotte, Major Shotte's wife, who sat on the balcony to view the beating of this "fiddler, this medicine man that nobody wants."

Major Shotte began mounting the balcony and paused to call out to the overseer, "Smith, get the bull cord and give it to Det to whip him." Then he went to the seats and sat next to Mrs Shotte.

Ti Nancy said she was a girl of thirteen years, a maid to Mrs Shotte, and had come out to the balcony to stand behind her mistress in case she needed anything. As the

Major sat, Det appeared walking to the whipping post. Smith handed him a whip the length of Ti Nancy's height plus a hand-breath more. He flexed the whip and moved towards Mohamed who was firmly tied to the post securely rooted in the lawn, which spread all around the great house yard.

Det, a tall giant of a Negro, dressed in short ragged trousers, stooping as if carrying a bag of potatoes on his shoulders and moving as if anxious to receive a prize for fancy whipping, stopped a pace on the back side of Mohamed and drew his outstretched hand to almost behind his back, whip outstretched.

Mohamed, in a voice expressive of fear, pain, anger and pleading shouted, "No Massa, Sah! I not do dat ting. I do nutting."

Lifting his eyes to the sky he cried, "Massa God, tell Massa Shotte I do nutting."

But Det spun his torso with his left hand outstretched, the whip striking across Mohamed's back from shoulder to shoulder making a sound as if a gunshot went off.

At the same instant Mrs Shotte shrieked in pain, "O God, Mercy!"

Major Shotte sprang up, grabbed his wife and yelled, "O God, stop!"

Mrs Shotte was bleeding from a cut from shoulder to shoulder as if the whip Det wielded had struck her, instead of Mohamed. Mrs Shotte in a voice full of anguish called out, "Let that man go! Leave him be! Do not whip him, for God's sake! Let him be."

A mule-rider fetched the doctor from Gardenville. The confusion and babble of voices subsided and silence ensued when the doctor and Major Shotte appeared on the balcony heatedly talking to each other with much gesticulating towards Mohamed who was still tied to the whipping post.

Then Major Shotte called, "Smith, cut him loose and let him sit at the office until the doctor and I get there."

At the office Major Shotte signed a paper on which the doctor wrote many words. This was handed to Smith with the instructions, "Take this man to the warden's office and give this paper to the ward officer. This is to free him and if he is seen on any part of this estate from today, you kill him."

Mohamed Brebnor was freed by registering the 'Note of Manumission' at the warden's office. Major Shotte ordered the slaves to lift and carry a one-room wooden house made of gru-gru board to a spot at Sheep Pen Ridge in Glenmorgin.

The house was carried that same evening and it was thatched with palm leaves before dark by eager and sorrowing slaves, and Mohamed Brebnor slept on the floor of that house, a deep sweet sleep of 'me not slave no more'.

This was the story told by Ti Nancy, the sister of Mohamed, as she lay dying at her one-room wooden house made of gru-gru board in Glenmorgin in the year 1930.

Chapter Four

Lazarus and the Rich Man

S lavery was abolished since 1834 and this was 1931. I was hopeful and anxious to see Richland Great House and the whipping post, they say, still stood on Liksill. So when Pa gave me a letter to take to Major Shotte, I anxiously placed the letter in a canvas bag, part of which I spread on the back of Anoo, our donkey, sprang on its back and trotted off on the two-and-a-half-mile journey to Richland Estate.

The day was bright and sunny. This was in the morning before the sun got hot. So I rode from the main road up the private road, a little less than half-mile to the back of the sprawling white, wooden building where there was a track leading between a brick oven and the kitchen.

"Morning Sah! Morning Ma'am!" I sang out, still sitting on Anoo.

This I did several times until the dogs set up a frightening chorus of barks, which stopped when a window was pushed out and a uniformed Negro woman snarled at me. "Shut you mout. Stap yuh noise. You want to wake up Mistress? Wha you want?"

I replied, "Please ma'am, mi father send mi wid a letter fuh Major Shotte."

Then she said, "Look, take yuh donkey back down a road and no make it shit pan Major Shotte lawn."

I spurred Anoo and went down to the main road and tied Anoo over the road bank so that she could graze until I got back. I then walked the distance back up to the window with the canvas bag folded on my left shoulder.

Again I called, "Morning ma'am," a few times until the uniformed woman stepped from a door she pushed open in my direction.

"Yuh deaf?" she hissed. "Shut up! Nuh make noise ah Major Shotte place. Put the letter heah," stretching a wooden tray toward me.

I put the letter on the tray, then she said, "Go siddung by dat mango tree," pointing to it, "and wait see if Major Shotte ha message fuh you carry back".

She disappeared into the house and I sat on a root that from its smoothness was certainly used as a convenient and comfortable seat. I waited, using my eyes to take in the grandeur of the great house: the beauty of the lawn, the white stones encircling the fruit trees and flowers, the spacious kennel in which the dogs lived, the quiet and cool breeze blowing all the while. You could see in the distance all around for miles from where the great house stood. I took this in, being in awe of wealth, power and whiteness of skin. The remembrance of where I lived, the house, the yard including the pigs' pen, the donkey stable and the neighbours' noises did something to my head, for since then to now the picture is vivid, down to the missing index finger on the left hand of the Negro woman.

The Negro woman reappeared through the door carrying a galvanized bath pan in front of her, clutching it with both hands. She passed about a foot in front of me and I smelled meat, roasted meat, and saw that the bath pan contained approximately, judging the size, twelve to fifteen pounds of doved beef. She headed for the dog kennel, opened the kennel door and put in all that doved beef for the three dogs to eat. She closed the kennel door, picked up the empty bath pan and disappeared into the house again.

Suddenly, something exploded inside of me, for water filled my eyes and I remembered Pa, Ma, my brothers and sisters, Nen, Happy, Ma Betsy and all the children in the village, how we all attend church, listen to the parson, and how we all prayed to God for everything we wanted, but God gave Major Shotte's dogs better house and food than He gave to us who went to church every Sunday and prayed, sometimes very loud and sometimes silent.

It was the first time, at age six going on seven years, that I began to understand why Pa kept quarrelling with my mother about poverty. Why he constantly explained that we had nothing but our strength and that the white man controlled things just to keep us poor, for us to work for them so that they can live a 'life in London' - that is, to live like a king with us his slaves, doing all the work. I saw dogs, Major Shotte's dogs, eating a meal such as I never saw or heard eaten by anybody in our village. I was angry with God. I was vexed with the parson. All of them were only telling lies.

The village ate meat twice per year: at Easter and at Christmas. The Estate would kill a cow at those times and after cutting off the choice parts they would sell the left-off and bones and tendons to the workers, and we never got more than one pound. It shocked me, seeing dogs eating choice meat and so much of it. I cried. I complained. And I cried some more. I walked down the hill. I got on Anoo's back and I sobbed and cursed and complained until I told God that he is a liar worse than Smiley who always is in jail.

On Sunday at Sunday School I recounted to the other children how I went to Richland Great House to carry a message and how Major Shotte feeds his dogs with great quantities of doved beef, while we were eating worse than dogs. Miss Henny told Ma how I was cursing Major Shotte and God in the churchyard and how Ma must correct my rudeness.

So when I went to her, held her frock and said, "Ma, I come from school," Ma struck me on my upper arm with the wet kitchen washing up rag, and in a vexed way said, "You making trouble in Sunday School. What wrong with you boy? You cursing white people? You cursing God, too? Go inside and take your Bible. Look for Luke Chapter 16 and read about Lazarus. You can read. Go read it and you will tell me about Lazarus and the rich man before you go to bed tonight. Go on!"

Inside I went, sniffling. I took off my school clothes, put on my bag-shirt, took the Bible, sat down by the back door and read about the rich man and Lazarus.

Pa came home from work and saw me sitting at the back door. He immediately recognized that I was being punished. So he asked my mother, "What Baily did?" She related how since I returned from carrying the message to Major Shotte I had been cursing white people and I even cursed God in the churchyard telling the other children how God is unfair and one-sided, how God likes white people and hates black people.

My father came to where I sat, looked at the page I was reading and asked, "What did the rich man ask Abraham?"

I said, "To allow Lazarus to give him some cool water." He nodded.

"And what did Abraham say?"

I replied, "Abraham told him no."

And my father continued, "Why you think Abraham told him no?"

"Because, Pa, that rich man is same as Major Shotte and them other white people. They take all the good and best things and leave us like Lazarus, poor with nothing."

Pa put out his hand on my head and rubbed it saying, "You're right, son. Just like we here, Lazarus couldn't get doctor to see about him. He gets sick and couldn't get medicine. Doctors in this island look after white people. When a doctor comes to the Health Office he brings a box full of bottles of bitter water. He gives the same to everybody. And is one injection and one pint of the bitter water and our sick do not get better. They always die. White people get from the doctor a different kind of medicine in different bottles and in little cardboard boxes. They, and the doctor as well, should all go to hell."

To this day I give full marks to my father for his wisdom in almost daily repeating to us, "Things to remember," he would say, "poverty and suffering are bosom friends whose aim is to destroy you.

They will kill you if you let them. They will kill you if you give in to them. If you fight them, the more you fight the stronger you will get and you will win."

But the village said of Pa and us that we were 'poor-great'. We were dirt poor humans refusing to be 'low class niggers' as the white children described us. We were "only" poor as Pa kept saying, "only poor."

Chapter 5

Pain Runs Deep

The thing that drove my father on was his superiority complex. He believed that he was better educated and of superior skills to every expatriate. Pa was tradesman contractor to them all. He put up their buildings, saw to the furnishing in their houses and helped with the bookkeeping and letter writing. He would refuse to eat in their kitchens or with the servants. He refused to do days' work and had two apprentices to carry his toolboxes whenever and wherever he worked, and he worked only as a contractor. For the villagers he worked with them like family - close family, for nothing most times.

The white folk described my father as "rude, out of place nigger, fresh nigger, upstart and that awful black clown."

But their servants and labourers and all the black folk in all the island were friendly to Pa and deeply respected him. He was literate and above average intelligence. Pa attended school held under the shade of a thick-leaved, sprawling mango tree, by a squat little man with a very long grey beard who it was said was the son of a slave that had lived some years with Massa Alefounder's father in England. The Alefounders owned approximately one-third of all Tobaccoc.

Pa wrote letters with a long, white feather pen and a pot of ink, for most of the folk around, including two white estate owners, Mr. Cathcart and Massa Beggs. He earned a little above existence wages. Pa was the leader of the Marcus Garvey Back-to-Africa Movement. Many, many people from outside the village came to talk with Pa. He used to preach to gatherings of visitors. Sometimes the white police officers would come to the house to tell my father to attend court to interpret for the indentured Indians since Pa wrote and read Arabic, spoke Hindustani and sang their songs.

The stories of injustice, unfair and inhuman treatment, together with the discriminatory practices I observed at school, at church and wherever and whenever I saw a white person, left me convinced that God, whose picture was a white man, lied to me. All people were not equal and people are not brothers. Only the white man was brother to other white men and they are God's children. God cared for them only and gave everything to them.

The very grass my pet goat ate belonged to the white man and if I forgot to take off my cap when I met any of them, I had to remove my goat from the estate lands.

In my youthful innocence, I began to dislike the white man. At first I used to tell Henry, Lowans, Bobo and Jambelly how I don't like white people and they would tell me how they don't like them, too. But that feeling intensified when Mr McLelland came from Europe to spend holidays. He, his wife and a small girl arrived on the island to stay with Reverend H P Q Banks, vicar of Saint Mary's and an evangelist from the mother country.

One day I had to carry a tray with papayas, ripe bananas and two pieces of sugar cane to the vicarage for Mrs McLelland. When I got to the yard in front of the house doorway I saw this huge white man who was not Reverend Banks so I said, "Morning Sah, Ma send these fruits for Mrs McLelland."

The white man who turned out to be Mr McLelland said, "Come here boy."

I answered, "Yes Sah," put down the tray in the yard and went to where Mr McLelland was standing.

He pointed to the branches of a golden apple tree some distance away and asked me, "What is that thing hanging there?"

I saw it was a nest of a corn bird we called 'bunyah'. They destroy your corn field, eating the young corn. As I began explaining to him he stepped towards where I stood, perhaps to get a better view, but he planted his foot on my left toes and I howled in pain pushing with all my strength to get him off my foot. Mr McLelland fell. Then all hell broke loose. The Negro yard boy leaped across the yard to the prostrate white man. The female housemaid set up a shrieking, bawling, that brought the whole house. Reverend Banks, the little white girl and the white dwarf dog, barking in a high pitched yap, yap, yap, all came running out.

Nobody asked me anything. McLelland pointing at me barked, "The little nigger pushed me down."

I directed my words to Reverend Banks, "Parson, Sah, the man burst mi toe!"

But Reverend Banks, God's representative in our village, lifted his right hand, delivered a blow across my ears and I saw fire in front of my eyes, then stars and I ran with all my strength straight home to Ma.

My left big toe was bleeding. I told Ma what happened and she took her hat to go over to the vicarage to find out. Luckily for me, Pa was in the ajoupa shoeing Mr Phillip's horse. Seeing that Ma doubted my story I went to Pa and told him what had happened.

Pa took my left foot on his lap, looked at the toe and said, as if to himself and the horse, "This toe, the blow come from on top of it; this is not stumping against something. They hit you?"

I said, "Yes Pa. Parson Banks nearly knock off my whole head. He give me one blow. I see a sheet of fire and my head still hurting me."

Pa looked concerned. "You go and sit down. I'm going over there myself."

Ma had already gone so Pa followed.

Ma and Pa returned to the house together. They did not speak. Pa was furious. Ma looked as if she had given up all her rights for peace and quiet. They had not spent much time at the vicarage and I had in my mind that Pa threatened to whip that Mr McLelland. Nobody said anything about the incident, not until Doctor Norris, a white doctor, rode into our yard on a horse with white on its four feet as if it had on white stockings.

Doctor Norris called out, "Where is the boy?"

Pa called, "Baily!"

I answered, "Yes, Pa, look me here."

The doctor dismounted. The horse stood still as if it was told not to move. The doctor lifted my left foot and turned it from side to side, twisting it and touching where the skin was torn. He mumbled something to himself, put my foot down, took his bag and with a cloth wiped my foot and put something from a small bottle on all my toes. My big toe felt as if it was on fire and I hollered.

My father suddenly said, "Doctor Norris, that foot, does it look like the boy stumped it against something?"

The doctor said, "No, the toes were crushed by a heavy weight."

"So, the boy is telling the truth that Mr McLelland crushed his foot?"

The doctor told Pa, "Look, man, it's no use you complain. Who you going to complain to? Why don't you keep your stupid black mouth shut and praise your God that the boy will not lose his foot?"

My father made a noise. It came from his belly. It contained rage and restraining effort. His hands moved as if in physical combat with a mortal enemy. The noise ended as if Pa was exhausted and defeated. He hung his head on his chest and I vowed revenge on all white people.

Chapter 6

Mrs Rodrix Boy

Pa's grandfather was a slave. Pa's father was born a slave. Pa is still a slave. He is always suffering. We, Ma, my sisters and my brothers had no fancy clothes. Ma had one pair of shoes since she got married. Pa had boots he made with wooden bottoms. But us children had only our ten commandments. We slept on the ground on crocus sacking mattresses stuffed with dried lavender grass. And we could always eat more.

At nights, before we lay down to sleep, we would all talk about the comforts and fine fancy things that lay strewn about the estate great houses. Sometimes Ma, through sobs and angry hand slapping on the sofa laths, would call to us as if begging. "I don't want not one of you to become labourer on the estate or servant for anybody. Learn your book and bring first in class and get out of this poverty barrier that them folk have us in."

Then Pa would put in his piece, "Education is in books. You all can read the same books them white children read. White people don't have more intelligence than us black people."

The more knowledge I acquired, the stronger my resentment towards the expatriates grew. Pa would tell us the things Father Stack, the Irish Catholic priest, would tell him. How he, Father Stack, read in books in Dublin and in England how Melchisedec, the Christ long before Jesus, in the Bible, was an African; how Solomon, the wisest man's mother was a Negro woman; how Egypt, Syria, Ethiopia, Palestine and Arabia had kings, princes and queens like the Queen of Sheba and warriors; how there was a University in Timbuktu and how he, Father Stack, understands how and why Pa wants to go back to Africa.

At age eight I was full of hate. One day my god-mother overheard me wishing aloud that Mr Hughes, the white overseer on the Brookeville Estate, should fall from his horse and break his neck.

She exclaimed in alarm and fear, almost crying, "Oh no, no! You mustn't say such wicked things. You are growing with hate. Stop thinking that way. There are white people that are good people. They are not all of them bad. Mr Hughes is a good, nice and generous man."

I bowed my head and said nothing but went to her side and placed my hand in hers and cringed in apology. She patted my head saying to me, "You must not hate people. You must forgive."

And she, Nen, as I used to call her, took me into her house and fed me cake - a big, big piece, and a large glass of the most heavenly drink I ever had. After this refreshment I forgot all about Hughes and Major Shotte, and the cake and milk drink started me dreaming of a life like Nen's with a nice house, cake and money.

Nen was a mulatto woman. Her grandmother was a house slave and her father was, they say, Captain Shotte.

She grew up in the great house and married a Portuguese white man. He died before I was born. He left her with lands, buggy, money and a little great house where the Health Office and the Post Office and the only telephone were. She was a fair, pretty and compassionate woman.

On reaching home I told Ma how Nen heard me saying Mr Hughes, who was passing on his horse, should fall and break his neck, how Nen scolded me, gave me a piece of cake she must have made for angels, how the cake melted in my mouth and how it was so sweet. I told her what Nen told me about forgiving the bad white people.

Ma asked me, "So you forgive white people?"

I said, "Yes Ma. Nen knows plenty things. She said the white people are not all bad. Mr Hughes is a nice man, and them children in school talk how Mr Hughes does give anything you beg him for. Even Miss Emelia could go inside Mrs Hughes house and sit on the big sofa and Mr Hughes don't put her out the house. Nen must be right; all white people not bad."

I felt somewhat liberated, at peace with my newfound understanding of human nature. Every race had good and bad people and I was happy knowing that there were good white people in the world. Then I asked Ma to send me to live with Nen for she had no children. Ma did not answer me.

From this time on my life changed. I began spending my daylight hours at Nen's house. I ran errands for her. I carried messages from the telephone and she would let me help with the mailbag. I became the envy at school and the self-appointed overseer at Sunday School. Miss Henny relied on me to 'carry news' on the other children. Now and again I would lose a fight on our way home after we left the church.

I looked nice in the clothes Nen bought for me. I had a pair of leather boots besides the alpargata I wore to church and school. The special brown leather boots were only for dressing up for Easter Sunday, Christmas or some notable occasion. I was so happy I began to love everybody. I was popular. The whole district called out to me as I ran to the houses to carry messages. The white people described me as 'Mrs Rodrix Boy'.

At school I was the brightest in class. I came first in everything but sports. I was treated by the teachers the same as the fair-skinned children. Nen used to visit the school. The headmaster, Mr Breck, would ring the bell and we would all keep still. Then he would ring it two times and everybody would stand. Then Mr Breck would say, "Say good morning to Mrs Rodrix." And the sixty three voices would shout, "Good morning Mrs Rodrix, Ma'am." Then one more bell and everybody would sit down again. Nen would then write in the logbook and leave after a long up-and-down handshake with Mr Breck.

I was happy as the months and years flew. When I was twelve years old, I sat the examination to go to the only secondary school in the island. How thrilled was I! I even daydreamed of asking Ruby, the brown-skinned daughter of Mr Chile, the white estate owner of Mount Dillon Estate, to go to Sunday School outing with me, if I passed to go to Grammar School. And, I passed.

Ma cried. Nen hugged me and kissed me. My brother grumbled at me how is now I will pamper-set and show myself. The boys in the village, when they heard that I would be going to Grammar School, stopped joking with me and would look at me funny-like. I felt no change in me. I was only happy. I loved everybody the same way.

Chapter Seven

Reading for the 'Bar'

I never got to go to Grammar School because Pa had written a letter to the governor, Sir Horace Archer Byath, complaining that he was beaten with a horse-whip by Police Inspector Swan. Pa explained to the governor that if he, Pa, had done something against the law, Swan had the authority to respond by locking him up.

But Pa had, in fact, done nothing at all to the white Inspector Swan or to anyone else.

What really happened was that Pa was walking on the public road, a wide road for cart and buggy to pass, when Inspector Swan let the horse push down Pa. He heard the horse clattering behind him, but the road was very wide so Pa didn't look back. When Pa, in anger and in pain, scrambled up he asked Inspector Swan if he and the horse were both blind. Swan proceeded to beat Pa with his horse-whip.

When Nen came to the house, it was a bad sign for she never visited. She would send for me or Ma or Pa. She never came unless it was sickness or death. So we all huddled together in the house corner waiting for Nen to share the bad news we expected.

Without greeting us, Nen said, "How unfair is this world? Mr Sauderson, the Inspector of Schools, knowing that Baily almost lives at my home and that I am responsible for him, called me on the telephone to tell me that the Inspector Swan gave him a letter stating that Baily is not to get the scholarship because Baily's family are trouble-makers. I tried to tell him no and to reason with him, but he says Inspector Swan told him that it is the governor who instructed him to write the letter."

Nen cried. Ma cried. I didn't cry. I ran into the bushes behind the house and up the hill to Hog Plum Ridge, sat down between some mulatto-plait grass and seethed as the realization of my broken dreams sank in. The old hatreds began to grow again.

Pa came home when the moon rose. I had just come from Hog Plum Ridge and stood by the front door hearing Ma repeat almost verbatim what Nen said on her visit. Pa only cleared his throat and said not a single word. That night there was total silence in the house.

Early next morning, before daybreak, I heard Pa waking up Ma.

Ma grunted and sat up asking, "Eh? What happen?" Pa said, "Ain't it have a private school in town?"

"Yes, Nen have a friend, Mr Makintosh, who have a private school, but it expensive and we don't have any money."

Pa exploded, "Damn it woman, if I have to steal to get those fees that boy going to Mr Makintosh School."

He continued, "You go and ask Nen to ask Mr Makintosh to take Baily and I am going to build things to sell. I will work like hell to find the money to pay. If I build a pig pen and get a pig, you going to have to mind it. Get some fowl egg and hatch them under Miss Mitti fowl. She have plenty. Let us try. I have to fight. A white man beat me up. I can't take him to court. The lawyer is white, the magistrate is white, the police white. Everybody white and I can't win them in court.

No black man in this country gets justice. They walk over you, they beat you, and you just have to take it? No. I'll fight them another way. Educate mi boy-children and if they take the education they can become lawyer or magistrate or doctor or police inspector. God is merciful. They can fight them."

Nen rose to the occasion. She not only got me a place at Mr Makintosh's School, she bought the clothes and paid the first term's school fee. She even arranged for me to stay at the people who rented her house in town not far from Mr Makintosh's School.

During my first term at school in town, Pa came to speak with Mr Mak, as everyone called him, and they discovered they had one thing in common. They were both followers of Marcus Garvey. A solid friendship was formed and Pa helped by doing repairs to the school.

Mr Mak took full charge of me. Sometimes he would call me to his quarters to eat with him. He liked my table manners and our quiet conversations about the injustices helped to refuel my dislike of expatriates, ignited by the loss of my scholarship.

Perhaps it was because I learned easily, for soon Mr Mak had me reading voraciously, telling me I could become a lawyer by reading, 'reading for the Bar'. So I read everything that I laid my hands on, from the Bible to the texts recommended for university students of the professions. Some which I, to this day, never understood. But I read and grew to like it.

There were new activities in and around the house. Ma cooked more to feed the apprentices Pa took on. Pa, the apprentices, my big brother, who was a monitor teaching in the school, and uncle Mallard, who Ma asked to come and help to get me to go to school, all worked every day except Sundays and in the nights sometimes.

Pa made trays from wood, cake pans and bread sheets from tin and galvanized iron sheets, but most of all he made wooden-soled boots that he called 'clogs'. Every male in the island sought a pair. Pa sold these clogs in other islands as well. The boot was shod with iron and a piece of metal on the tip. The wooden sole carried indentations to accommodate the instep and ball of the foot. And, it was very washable. It made a crunching sound as one walked in them, "Croow, croow, croow, croow," it said. These shoes lasted a very long time.

Funny, I never knew my father's correct name until one day Father Stack, the Irish Catholic priest, left a letter for my father and the address read, 'John Ecclesiastes', Brookeville. I handed the letter to Pa when he came home. He looked at it, looked at me and laughed.

As he tapped the letter he said, "I stopped calling myself Ecclesiastes since I was twelve years old. I call myself 'Iron'. I am John Sardona Iron. You are Baily Iron. Don't go calling yourself Ecclesiastes. People will laugh at you."

The letter read:

Dear John,

You are always poking fun at me that I am a beggar and a prayer. Yes I pray all the time and I beg when I have to. Yesterday at the magistrate's house I begged for you and I prayed. Nearly all the estate owners were there at

Meeden's birthday party and you were the topic. The Police Inspector brought it up how you wrote to the governor and how the governor pissed on you. They gave you a character I know you do not have but nobody, not one of them, will listen to me. They admit that you are educated, intelligent, a master tradesman and skilful, but you are a Negro trying to equal yourself with white folk with your acquired fine manners and speech. They have decided not to give you any more work and believe that you will, when you feel the pinch, make trouble of one sort or another and they will then see you go to jail. I write this to you to warn you, for I am your friend. You must look out for yourself.

Peter Stack

It was this letter from Father Stack that drove my father to superhuman effort. He built a house on land that Nen bought for him after the estate owner refused to sell Pa any land. And he worked even harder than before.

Chapter 8

Greater Expectations

After some four years, at age seventeen, I passed the London Matriculation exam. People, particularly school teachers, congratulated me and encouraged me to continue studying. It was an achievement for the school and Mr Mak's voice took on an inflection that ended always with an aspirated "heh heh." It was the first London Matriculation pass that the whole island achieved. Nen cried, clapping her hands for joy. Ma groaned that evocative gut expression that only us black people know. For us, black folk, heartfelt joy is conveyed with silent tears and the guttural groan.

Within days of receiving the examination results I became a hero, a champion, a messiah expected to change the village and the island from downtrodden sufferers to people that others noticed and respected. Everybody kept on asking, "What you going become? What you want to be? Is what you going study for now? Look we doctor boy." Miss Mitti and Ma Betsy cried as if something serious happened. Bo Rooshan lifted me off the ground and nearly strangled me in an embrace. He whispered to me, "Boy, we need a bright lawyer to stand up for we."

Reverend Banks, the parson who, years ago, nearly knocked my head off my neck, strode into our yard about two weeks after the exam results were announced. I sucked my teeth the way how we Negroes show contempt for a distasteful anybody.

Ma spoke through gritted teeth, "Manners boy, he is the Lord's anointed."

My disgust immediately swung to the beaming smile of a practised hypocrite, "Good morning, Vicar," I called.

"Oh, there you are, the very lad I've come to see and his dear mother who has never missed a single communion service. I hope I see you very well, dear heart," he called across to Ma who was coming away from the water barrel drying her hands with the tail of her calico dress.

"Thank you, Vicar. I am so and so with the help of the good Lord".

I shook the vicar's hand. It was the proper thing to do since he stretched out his whole limb as if to keep me some distance from the rest of him.

"How are you, boy? You've not only grown since I last saw you but you show signs of soon becoming a man to reckon with. Your head, shoulders and arms are like a fighter's torso! Even your eyes tell of an alertness seldom seen."

I parried with a blatant lie, "Your kindness is, as your visit to our humble dwelling, a great pleasure. I am sorry my father is not at home."

He smiled. "I've come to have a little talk with you, not your father. I hope he is very well?"

I made no reply but handled the bench that was in front of the house, offering the vicar a seat. He gestured refusal but said, 'Thank you. You sit."

So I sat and gave Vicar Banks my full attention. Ma stood a way off, busy with a part of her dress that hung from the hem of the skirt as if it got torn by the drying of her hands.

The vicar smiled as he observed her and said to me, "I hear tell that you've passed a great exam and will be going on to higher studies."

"Yes, sir. I was lucky to pass the exam, but I'm not going on to higher studies. I do not know what I'm going to do as yet."

"That's what brought me here," he said, still standing as if in a hurry to go and needing to speak quickly.

The vicar went on, "I was speaking with His Lordship, the Bishop, the other day and he is quite keen on having Negroes who show evidence of ability to learn, becoming ministers of the Anglican Church. On hearing of your success at the examinations I decided to offer you a bursary to a theological college in England. What do you think?"

"Up on Hog Plum Ridge." He frowned.

"Somebody trouble you?" Pa knew that whenever there is a problem or something on my mind I would head for Hog Plum Ridge to 'ponder his mind' as Pa would say.

"Only Parson Banks come today to offer to send me to England to study to become a parson."

"So what you told him?" asked Pa.

"I told him no because parsons like to strike little boys without finding out if they deserve the blow."

My father laughed and laughed, until I began wondering if what I said in answer to him was really funny. But as Pa spoke I felt good inside and understood his laughter.

Pa slapped his leg holding on to the stable's rail with his left hand and talked, as if telling his thoughts.

"I knew it! My prayers are answered. I knew it. Parsons don't fight they pray and beg. I knew it. You hit back at the priest for striking you years ago. You struck the first blow for justice. You will be a good lawyer. You make up your mind yet?"

I answered, trying to sound and look determined, "Yes Pa, on the hill today I come to feel that everybody I know, the black people, Mr Makintosh, Teacher Ridley, Manga

Waite, Gangang, Blessie, Sa Mice and even half-whites, like Nen Rodrix, would all want me to help the black people that are suffering and to stand up for them and to speak up for them. Only a lawyer can do those things and talk back to the white man or anybody. So I decided I want to go to read for the Bar. I want to be useful to the village, to the island and to you, Pa. You said many times, 'if you're not useful you're useless'. Mr Mak used to tell us that God didn't make anything useless. Everything God made has purpose. That if you don't have purpose in this life you become purposeless and useless to everybody. Whenever I hear people complaining and crying out, it is as if they are asking me to do something. Pa, only as a lawyer do I see myself being able to help. Big job and money are important to many people, but it is the mind that is the most important. If you can get people to use their minds, money becomes unimportant and people can make life easier without the white man and his money. If I am a lawyer I can fight for justice in and outside the court. People will listen and then I can help."

There ensued a silence. Pa was looking at me. He stared as if I were something he saw and heard for the first time. He moved closer to me, held my hand and dropped to the ground on one knee and with tears in his eyes said, "God, my father, you hear what this my son just said. Bend your ears and hear me as I cry. Help him, and help me, O God, to help him that he could help bring justice to us a suffering people. Please God, hear us and be with us day and night and always. Amen and Amen and Amen."

Next day Pa and I took the bus 'Eastern Star' from Brookeville in to town and walked straight to Mr Mak's Private Boys School. It was a Saturday morning and Mr Mak ought to have been out exercising his shiny black mare. Instead, he was standing at the school's entrance as if waiting for someone.

Seeing us he called, "Hello father Iron and son Iron. This is a great day for this unexpected visit tells me that something is very important. Come in, come in. Let us go upstairs to my quarters."

He led us to the dining table. Pa sat across from Mr Mak and I sat at the head or the tail, I don't know which. The housekeeper, Miss Mabel Harper, was out to the market shopping. We were alone, the three of us. Mr Mak got back up and walked to the door and closed it. If Mabel came up the stairs we would hear.

Mr Mak said to Pa, "Seeing you with Baily says no to a tot before chat, so business it is then. Let's fire away."

Pa fired the first and opening shot. "How much money to send this boy to wherever he has to go to study?"

Mr Mak rubbed his chin and kept slowly moving his jaw up and down as if he was chewing the question, eventually asking Pa, "You know it is to England you have to send him?"

Pa said, "Yes, but where in England is the school for lawyers?"

Mr Mak replied, "There are four Inns of Court, but students do not stay at these Inns. They have to live elsewhere. About the living, I will make enquiry. About the Inns, I will get that information from the magistrate. His boy is at my school so the father and I get along pretty well."

"But," interrupted my father, "it is about the amount of money I want to find out."

"The tuition at the Inns of Court School of Law will be approximately eighty guineas per year for four years. Living accommodation may be in the vicinity of twenty-five guineas per year. Let us say then that the whole thing should cost about one hundred and twenty guineas per year including books, but excluding clothes and pocket money."

Pa looked around as if to ensure that no one was within earshot. Satisfied, he said, "I have four hundred pounds buried. Nobody but I know where. I was planning for years to buy one of the estates on this island. If the white man knows that I aspire to be an estate owner like them, they would find ways to stop me. This boy's education can do more for the people and me than an estate. So, my brother Makintosh, join with me and let us send him off. You make all the arrangements, please, and let us keep this in silence as the grave."

There was pleasant talk for a bit until Mr Mak brought out a bottle he said the magistrate sent as a gift to him.

Pa looked at it and exclaimed, "Man, that's a good one. It is 'Prince Charlie', a good Scottish whiskey."

The conversation became louder and with laughter as Pa made me relate to Mr Mak the conversation with Vicar Banks offering me the priesthood and my reply to him.

My plans for my departure to England were interrupted by the unsettling repercussions of a disastrous war. Basic food items such as rice, flour and potatoes were rationed and we had to rely solely on our agricultural produce. Our governor regulated the price of all commodities to prevent vendors overcharging. The black folk on our island and those on neighbouring islands all had to work twice as hard during World War II. The already depressing living standards worsened and the villagers were desperate. It was because of this that Ma, Pa and Nen encouraged me to accept an opportunity to travel to South America for work.

Chapter Ten

Delays and Diversions

I was forced to grow up quickly in Venezuela. It was my first time away from my family and friends and I had to rely totally on my own judgment and the principles and values taught to me by Ma, Pa, Nen and Mr Mak.

Two experiences in particular intensified my faith and gave me an understanding of the compassion that some white people were capable of. They prepared me for my sojourn in England and removed many of the judgements formed solely as a result of the injustices I had witnessed in Tobaccoc.

After landing in Puerto La Cruz, I managed to secure work as a tool-pusher in a company that was putting up an oil refinery. Because I quickly became bilingual I was promoted to warehouse-man and was put in charge of Tools and Equipment.

I ran the entire department and was responsible for all goods received from the port and the airport. To all appearances, I did a good job until one Henry Rheinman appeared at my office and declared that he was sent to take over the warehouse and I was to be his assistant. I conceded and we enjoyed an amicable working relation-ship until Rheinman brought his nephew, Carlos, from Texas. He was bilingual also and Mr Rheinman told me I was to teach Carlos my job. I replied, "Yes sir," but did nothing.

After a few days Rheinman asked me why was I not teaching Carlos the warehouse procedures. I told him that he should not expect me to teach somebody to do the job

Tears were in my eyes as I explained, "Sir, I do not know what sins I am guilty of but God is striking me with a very heavy hand and I am at his mercy."

The man surveyed the vehicle and the wheels, then looked at me intently. He went to his car, opened the trunk and returned to my truck. He picked up the two wheels, put them in his trunk and started his car. I watched, both puzzled and in awe, as he turned the car around and drove off towards Barcelona ignoring everything I had been muttering.

About twenty-five minutes afterwards the man and woman drove up and stopped. He came out of the car, opened the trunk and took out the two wheels with new tyres on them. He placed them at the side of my vehicle. I quickly pushed my hands into my pockets pulling out coins I had left, which did not amount to much.

The man protested, "No! No! No! I want no pay! All I want in return for my humble efforts is that as you meet people, all people, you be kind to them, for we are all just people on the same road to the hereafter."

I was overwhelmed with gratitude and deeply moved by his kindness. I hollered and bawled and cried as that man and his companion drove away. I eventually put a new tyre on and slowly drove to Santa Inez. Along the way I reasoned. One white man virtually kicked me out of my job, now another white man put me back on the road. This white man never said, "White people you meet." He said 'all people'. Yes, he said, "We are all just people on the same road to the hereafter."

* * *

I returned to Tobaccoc a fluent writer and speaker of Spanish, and knowledgeable about marine technology and everything related to ships and sailing through work experience. In the aftermath of the war, we took to re-establishing stability and some semblance of what was regarded as normal life.

During all this time I never lost sight of my dreams of becoming a lawyer and defender of my people. Neither did Pa, Ma, Nen or Mr Mak. After several months of documents being sent and resent to England, we received a letter of acceptance stating that classes were due to commence in October 1951.

I saw a side of my father that left an indelible impression on me during those months leading up to my

At one time I chuckled to myself as I wondered if the white people in Europe had told the sea to prevent me somehow from getting to England. That thought quickly vanished, however, when a young white steward came and suddenly grabbed me just as a wave hit the ship on the side near to the bow and a mountain of water fell on the deck violently drenching all of us, black and white alike.

I remembered then what Nen had said to me the night before I left. She said, "Baily, my dear, dear boy, remember that this world has many nice people, black people, white people. England will show you many good white people." Then memories of the Masonic Chief in Venezuela and the white couple who replaced my flat tyres flashed before me.

I could feel the gratitude filling my entire being as I looked at the sailor boy who didn't care about my colour. Had he not grabbed me in the nick of time, that water would have surely washed me overboard and then, goodbye forever. He saved my life.

Yes, there were many nice black and white people and this good young man had not thought twice about helping me. I could not have asked for a more timely or better confirmation of Nen's words. Any residual resentment that

I may unknowingly have had towards white people was released on this eventful day.

Until I reached Liverpool ten days after nearly being washed overboard, my mind kept revolving around one thought. It kept always coming back. "You're going to England to study to become a lawyer." Even after my arrival, this continued to engulf me to the point of paranoia. Of enormous awe-filled significance to an untutored youth coming from a background of emptiness, categorized by the descriptive word 'underdeveloped', is the false perception of a personal lack of ability. His presence as a human unit means nothing to anyone and his functions - physical and otherwise - are neither recognized nor needed by anyone.

It was a grey and cold October. London did not meet my expectations. They were fuelled by a child's observations of wealth and opulence as displayed at the estate houses in Tobaccoc, and as I explored my surroundings what was unfolding was much to the contrary. I was surprised to see white people doing menial jobs and to meet some who were barely literate. My search for affordable student accommodation led me to homes to know about 'race' and 'prejudice'. Each day, after the midday break, I raced to a different library. I even went to the British Museum. It was a massive disappointment to discover that the literature on 'race' was purely scientific and not slanted to the practice of prejudicial relationships among men. The matter of 'prejudice' lay in the area of human behaviour and is based solely on the mindset of the individual. The physical discriminatory practices are not founded on factual truths but on emotion both unreasonable and unjust.

Armed with nothing but myriad reported cases of racial discrimination and personal experience, I truthfully told the expectant white faces looking at me that evening that the only talking point surfacing from a deliberate research into the embarrassing question of racial prejudice is 'the ignorance of a racist'. As I spoke, I noticed that I had no feelings of resentment, no hurt triggered by my recollection of the injustices witnessed during my early life in Tobaccoc. I articulated effortlessly, with pride, confidence and a sense of awareness and liberation.

I explained that there is not a single statistic to support the inferiority in every area of human endeavour of the Chinese, the Jew, the African, or the Amerindian. Medical science can find nothing to support the prejudicial statement that African or Jewish or Eskimo blood is different from the blood of the English people. That Hannibal, the Negro general, overran Europe and so did Genghis Khan. There was a University in Timbuktu when England was inhabited by ignorant club-toting, wife-beating forest dwellers. I spoke of the Queen of Sheba, of Cleopatra, and of King Jaja of Opobo, whom the British exiled from his Kingdom in Nigeria. I explained how King Jaja died broken hearted by reason of the treachery of the British.

There was some other Baily speaking to these young folk at Woodbine. I forgot myself and some inner person, not the usual me, was telling them that what produced the rape and underdevelopment of Africa by the heads of France, Britain, Germany, Spain, Portugal and Holland was the egoistic drive to have more for themselves. These atrocities were committed first by the heads and their courts, then the courtiers, the noblemen, the adventurers and the traders. Even the criminals were deported to the colonies as punishment.

All these were and still are interested in their personal comfort, fortune and power. They lied and promised, made treaties, used military might and the Christian religion, and they established a superiority by force of arms. Those they couldn't defeat in battle they conquered by trickery. In addition, the Europeans had to ensure their superiority by condemning and obliterating the history of us African peoples. They classified humanity into black and white. They introduced favouritism to the lighter shade of pink and condemnation to the point of downright brutality on the dark skin. Everything dark was inferior. Skin colour as a yardstick crept into the education system, the economic system, the social stratification, and even into religion.

I told them of Reverend Banks knocking my head so hard that I saw flames before my eyes, and prejudicially, without evidence or investigating anything, coming to the conclusion that I was a young savage, aged seven years, doing violence to his guest. He failed to appreciate that the pain caused by his guest stomping on the foot of a little boy created the reaction to push away the cause of the pain - a full grown, corpulent man standing on my foot. I told them of the horsewhipping the Inspector of Police gave my father for not getting out of the way of the Inspector's horse. How my father hollered at him, "Are you blind, man?" and ended up being beaten.

I remembered stopping abruptly after saying to them, "If your ego - your idea and feeling - perceives that you are the most important living being next to God, then you must justify and demonstrate that belief and feeling. You look to the differences among people to see how high up the ladder to God you are. So the Chinese's eyes are funny and their skin is yellow, the Amerindian lives off the land without farming and has a strange language and way of life, the Negro is black and must be dirty. Everything infers that white people are better than all other peoples because their skin is white. You can get the Negro riled by continuous maltreatment but prejudice against other races is not natural. Do not be surprised if one day he fights you to stand among all men and establish his right not to be an animal but to be a man among men."

The result of this research and lecture was a total transformation of my psyche. It reinforced my belief in Christianity as explained by the white Anglican priest, Leonard Wilson, who consistently taught us kids that Paul of Tarsus preached the mission of Jesus, the Christ, that all men are born equal and man must do to others what they would like others to do to them. These are the foundation rocks on which God built the universe.

The Lecture

I understood that colour and texture of hair, colour of skin, shape of nose, thickness of lips and slant of eyes are not characteristics of any body of people. And if we are to be guided by nature's functionings, the teachings and preachings of the seers, prophets and patriarchs, together with the myths and customs underpinning our civilization, we find our sole entitlement to existence is 'usefulness', animated existence towards purpose as opposed to uselessness.

Chapter 13

Mission Accomplished

On the 7th November, 1956 I was admitted to the Bar in England at a grand ceremony at the Middle Temple Inn of Court. I received my rolled up parchment but was not at all thinking of being proud or elated. My thoughts were with my folk at Brookeville. Their thoughts were with me, longing for me to come home to make them proud and happy for the result of their sacrifice and confidence in me. I was counting the days until I could board the train and the *SS Vayala* for home.

It must have been the blue bag with my name embroidered on it that the steward saw in the cabin, for at sea the next day a white man came and sat at my table and said in a very friendly tone, "So what will it be? Politics? Or defender of the poor?"

I said, lying, "I don't get you."

"You're finished studying. You're returning home. Your thoughts must be on what you're going to do when you get home. Politics?"

"You must give me some answers before I answer you. First, where are you going? Next, what you think I should do when I get home? What side are you on? Politics or poor people?"

The fellow laughed, leaned back in the chair and said, "I am Selman Shotte. My father, Major Shotte, is not very well these days and I am going to Richland in Tobaccoc where he lives. And, I am on the side of the poor people. You look, you have the look of a lawyer and I will hope that we are going to the same island where we can be friends."

I said jestingly, "When a white man is searching for a friend among the blacks, something is wrong with that white man. The world is a white world. The whole world is his friend, the white world. When he looks to a Negro proffering friendship something sure is wrong. Tell me, why me?"

Selman let a few seconds pass before he spoke, "Look friend, for the past five years the world has changed dramatically. Black folk like yourself are getting educated by the droves. Have you not seen the number of black students all over London? They are going home one by one. And hell is going to break loose one day. I am choosing to be on the side of the hell-raisers. I need friends among the poor for they shall inherit the earth of my father's estate. I see it coming."

"Not for a very long time," I replied. "The white man uses his intellectuals to study and plan for the non-whites. The non-whites are the labourers and consumers of goods made by the white man with the raw materials the labourers themselves produce. They virtually buy the products their labour produces. The white man has put the systems together and enforces them. It is a well-knit, well-designed, well-implemented, well-enforced network and the labourers can't match the organizational ability and skill of the white players on the world economic chessboard. Only, as the Chinese say, "The little fish will get smart in order to survive the ravages of the big fish." Educate the little fish. Education develops the mind and it is the mind that dominates the physical. So, you see, hell is bound to break its bounds one day to come."

Breakfast was served and the conversation drifted to what other peoples in the world eat for breakfast. I felt a sadness remembering that my people at home ate whatever was edible and available, sometimes nothing at all.

After fifteen long days at sea interspersed with profound conversations with my new friend, Selman, we finally made it back home to my beloved island. I was delighted to find a father demanding, "How was it?" and a mother smiling permanently and virtually dancing about offering cake, sorrel, ginger beer, roast pork, roast peccary and creamed yam. The villagers were ecstatic too, and one by one approached for a handshake, some a hug.

It was with a feeling of pleasurably expressed satisfaction that the gathering at the welcome home party heard the lawyer say, "Let me thank every single one of you for the many twenty-four pence (one shilling) I received from you that helped me to come home to you to help." The crowd clapped and shouted, "Praise God, Praise God, Praise God," for a long time.

The most enthusiastic of the crowd that had gathered to welcome me home was my cousin, Jabez Shotte, the policeman. He was a favourite among the villagers for they had heard stories of how he arrested and charged two white men for embezzling the moneys of Richland Estate, owned by Captain Shotte. White Captain Shotte and Jabez' father shared the same father which made them half-brothers. Their father's mother was sister to my grandmother. Jabez was respected because he was literate, had sat and passed the London Matriculation examination but could not get a job as a teacher. All the schools were governed by expatriates who made sure that the bright black boys be 'kept in their place'. So Jabez became a literate, respected, black, efficient police constable.

The wife of Colonel Proctor of the Police Department, Maizie by name, had opened a tea shop where she sold tea, cakes, milk and fruit drinks to the white community. Blacks could go in and buy things but could not sit or stay there to eat or drink. They were put outside. A villager or peasant farmer who owned a cow was encouraged to sell his milk to Miss Maizie's tea shop. An unwritten policy emerged that milk sold other than to Miss Maizie had to be tested or the seller could be charged for selling adulterated milk.

PC Jabez was on the main street on his way to the office one morning when a white woman stepped in front of him forcing him to an abrupt halt.

She said, "Constable, where are you going?"

Jabez replied, "On police business, Ma'am."

"Are you not taking milk samples?"

"No Ma'am," he replied, "and even so it's none of your business Ma'am. If you want to make a report, tell me and I'll see what I can do."

To this the woman shrieked, "Oh, oh!" as if struck. "You are nothing but a stupid idiot in policeman's uniform. I'm going to have you disciplined."

Jabez replied in a somewhat authoritative voice, "Ma'am, I do not know you and you are insulting me. If you continue that behaviour on the street, I will arrest you."

The woman uttered a bawl-like, "Whaaat? Arrest me?"

A white man ran from the tea shop, grabbed Jabez in the street and spun him around. Jabez stumbled and managed to avoid falling by gripping the white man's shirt. An embittered Jabez drew his fist aiming for the head of the white man. Two Negroes ran from the gathered crowd, pushed between Jabez and the white man and held on to Jabez' hands. It was suicidal to strike a white person.

Jabez quickly regained his composure, pulled out his pocket book and proceeded to question the onlookers. He was told that the woman was Miss Maizie, owner of the tea shop and wife of Colonel Proctor, Assistant Inspector General, and that the white man who assaulted him was Miss Maizie's brother, Captain Roy Aston of the Regiment up at Fort David.

Jabez returned to the police station and attempted to report the incident. Before he was able to utter a word Sergeant Major Bash gave instructions for him to be confined to Barracks by order of the governor, Sir Danglin Foote, for being insolent to Miss Maizie Proctor. The following day Jabez Shotte was dishonourably discharged from the Police Force of Tobaccoc.

I understood Jabez' enthusiasm at my return when I heard his story as he quoted every word of the tea shop incident with anger, swearing that at last these perpetrators of injustice who destroyed the lives of innocent, well-meaning black people would yield the fruits of their misdeeds.

Jabez virtually demanded my taking Miss Maizie and Governor Danglin Foote to the courts to let the village and the whole island see justice done. My entire family agreed and clapping of hands, cheering voices, glee-filled laughter, including calls from unnoticed bystanders peeping through the windows, sealed the unanimous, vociferous agreement to take the incident and everyone concerned in Jabez' discharge to the courts.

The welcoming home party continued late into the night with most guests leaving at about second cock-crow at one in the morning. About ten of us remained. We were seated everywhere, anywhere, and I was urged to tell them everything about everything since the day I left Tobaccoc.

Ma asked if I had fights in England and if whites behaved the same as those here. I explained that indeed there is a prejudice in England against black people, but mainly due to ignorance. The people in England did not know people of black skin, but once they got to know you they treated you just as they treat their own white folk. I eventually told them of my lecture to the Woodbine Literary and Debating Club and the conclusions I drew from it.

We chatted endlessly, way into the night. This continued for about three days until Mr Joshua Smith, a local white lawyer, agreed to present me to the Bar. The following morning I was ceremoniously admitted to practise at the Bar of the Islands, which included Tobaccoc, Trinity, Lagrine and Misratte.

Mr Joshua Smith, at my admission to the Bar, remarked to the assembled lawyers that I was son of the John Iron who was horsewhipped by Inspector Swan and that he, Joshua Smith, was "sure to defend the Inspector since John Iron now has his own lawyer and a black one, too, to prosecute our boy Swan." Instantly I remembered the governor, who deprived me of the scholarship to Secondary School and who had instructed the very Inspector to communicate the denial.

Timidly, I ventured a remark. "Mr Smith," I called out, my voice trembling with emotion, "these courts and the laws are aimed at justice!"

Smith replied, almost shouting at me, "Whose justice? Yours or ours?" I held my anger and waited to sign the oath, for the judge had already hurriedly retreated.

Next day the only newspaper of the Island, *The Trumpeter*, carried a picture of me all robed and wigged, no smile, just standing there, full length, looking ahead. Below was what appeared to be an excerpt of a speech I never made.

"Thank you my Lord, for admitting me to practice. I will endeavour to serve the cause, the enslavement of my forefathers."

What I had said was, "Thank you my Lord for the kind advice and encouragement. I worship at the shrine of justice and pledge to you, before you and this August gathering, to do my best. Thank you Sir."

To provide sustenance, particularly physical sustenance, to the intelligent, able-bodied human is to remove the *'joie de vivre'* from his contemplations, if he accepts the role he is forced to take. The interlocking of use with purpose is the character of function, and life or living is functional activity. One is predisposed to usefully function to fulfil purpose. It is not a matter of survival to exist. One exists to survive. It is useful existence towards purpose that justifies survival.

* * *

The legal system functions on one resident Judge of a High Court, three magistrates of a lower court, a visiting, non-resident Appeal Court and a Privy Council resident practically functional in Great Britain.

From a room divided into three poky rooms I began practice using a female cousin as clerk and receptionist. She found, on the very first day, three matters in the criminal court. Two of these were postponed for summoning of witnesses, but the third brought me almost instant fame as the best begging lawyer the courts ever had before it.

The magistrate was an expatriate - married, wealthy, with no children. The defendant was one of the poorest of our community. Her appearance bordered on theatrical. She had dressed for the occasion in an ill-fitting, deformed straw hat on a head displaying erect pigtails above a dress almost transparent through many washings, supported by two very straight legs, shod in ill-fitting alpagartas. She stood before 'Her Worship', tears streaming silently down.

I addressed the magistrate. "The plea is 'guilty', Ma'am. But I wish to be heard in mitigation."

"Yes, Mr Iron, you may proceed."

"Ma'am," I began, "My first appearance before you, is a very unhappy experience. It has nothing to do with the Court or its officers, Ma'am, but with this guilty defendant. She, Ma'am, has not only brought back to me days I had hoped to forget, but she forcibly portrays the dilemma, which Your Worship, and indeed myself, face, in our attempt to do justice. Look at her, Ma'am, a picture of poverty, obvious lack of knowledge, destitution and want. She, in her ignorance, Ma'am, took two dresses from the hundreds her Mistress has in a closet. She believed that the Mistress could not possibly have missed them. So she removed them and hung them on a nail behind the door in the maid's room. The Mistress discovered them there and demanded, 'Who gave these to you?' Whereupon this simple-minded soul confessed that she took them because, 'Mistress have so many an I have nuttin to put on.' The Mistress called the police. Justice says to us, Ma'am, we must show mercy to the poor. Just look at her Ma'am. Poverty, want and ignorance stand there before you begging for mercy. She can say nothing, but her tears speak."

At that point I became awkwardly emotional, took out my handkerchief and wiped a cloudiness, which settled before my eyes.

The magistrate took off her glasses and wiped her eyes saying at the same time, "Yes, Mr Iron, I understand. Young woman, you are free to go. Just a minute, Mrs Anderson, do you want the dresses?"

The virtual complainant said, "No Ma'am, let her have them, please."

The audience in the well of the Court clapped in applause and the police sergeant and two constables, in chorus, shouted, "Silence! Order!" until the applause abruptly ceased.

In England they taught me at Law School that 'justice' was the sole objective of the practice of the legal profession, and that laws, rules of practice and procedure are aids to attain justice. The tutors stressed that justice cannot be taught as a subject. If one subscribes to a religion or to religious practices, or if one is guided by principles on which hang the concepts of morality, then justice underlies your interpretation of what is morally right, correct, true, good or otherwise. Nonetheless, civilised people agreed broadly on what is right and what is wrong, what is therefore acceptable and what is not, and the laws reflect those formulations, or ought to.

From my first day as a professional, I knew that I had landed in trouble for I never got out of thinking my religion, my conscience and the warning advice given us by Sergeant Sullivan at Law School had combined to create in me, a mindset built on the concept that one's life belongs to the agent that created it and that life is based on and has for objective, truth and justice.

CPSIA information can be obtained
at www.ICGtesting.com
Printed in the USA
FFOW02n1917230315
12075FF